Walking in Light, Living in Love

DOTHULA BARON

Walking in Light, Living in Love
Copyright © 2024 by Dothula Baron

All rights reserved. No part of this publication may be reproduced, distributed, or transmitted in any form or by any means, including photocopying, recording, or other electronic or mechanical methods, without the prior written permission of the author, except in the case of brief quotations embodied in critical reviews and certain other non-commercial uses permitted by copyright law.

Library of Congress Control Number: 2024916469

ISBN
978-1-964982-36-6 (Paperback)
978-1-964982-37-3 (eBook)

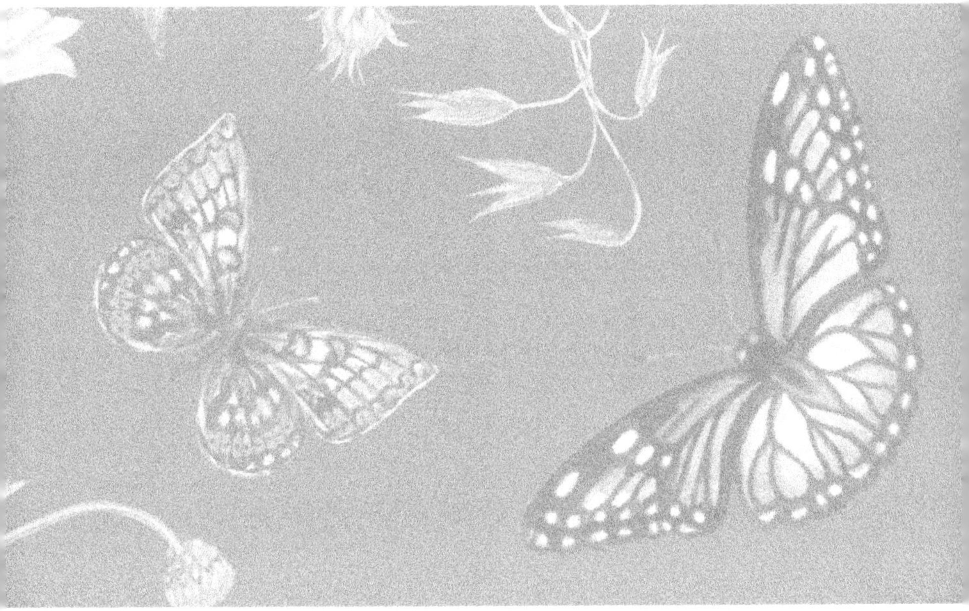

Table of Contents

Preface vii
Acknowledgements ix
Introduction xi

My Spiritual Life: Who I Am 1
Intuition: Listening to the God Within 6
Empowerment: Knowing the Divine 13
Love: The Most Powerful Force 20
Healing Oneself: Tools for Change 29
Healing the Planet, Changing the World 37
Lifelong Learning: Sustaining Peace 40
Sex and Intimate Relationships 46

Conclusion: Valuing One's Worth
and Living on Purpose 49

Preface

We are all moving through this vast universe, and as we travel, we are drawn to certain people, things, and experiences that we must stop to appreciate. It is like we have no choice. If we fail to partake (or "drink the wine"), we get other chances. Sometimes, we miss opportunities and go in other directions (go against the grain), but if we are wise, we soon get back on course. Life is like a smorgasbord (so much to experience), but if we are discerning, we choose wisely, accepting those experiences that feed us and that are for our highest good, and that either bring us joy or bring us pain. It is through these periods of discomfort that we grow, we *become*. We rise into the best that we can be—into joyful, loving, gracious beings filled with love and light.

Acknowledgements

This book is dedicated to my mother, Vinnie Baron, who transitioned in 1974, when I was only twenty-five. It was after she departed that I began to take my writing seriously. It was then that I began to feel her presence whenever I sat down at a typewriter, later at the computer, and in almost every other realm of my life. She has been my guide, my guardian, my light. In fact, her spiritual teaching started when I was a child. We were Catholic, but she subscribed to Unity's *Daily Word*. I read every issue. Later she explained that she belonged to the Rosicrucian Order, a society devoted to the study of metaphysics. She also identified herself as a psychic. Through the years, I learned to appreciate her teachings and allowed them to permeate my being. Even after her passing, I felt her guiding and directing me. I am forever grateful for having her as my teacher. Thank you, Mother, for making me who and what I am. Amen!

I also want to dedicate this book to Evelyn Coleman, author of several children's and young adult books, including two American Girl mysteries. She is my college friend, dorm mate, and "sister," who has been with me on this journey and appreciates who and what I am. She is my muse. Thank you!

Introduction

On Friday, February 10, 2017, I was admitted to the ICU (Intensive Care Unit) for a thoracic aortic aneurysm. I had had back and chest pain all day long. It was excruciating. By the time I saw my primary physician at her office, she ordered me to immediately go to the emergency room and called ahead to let them know was on my way.

It took me awhile to wrap my brain around what that meant. When the vascular specialist first told me that I had a thoracic aortic aneurysm, he also explained that with the surgery, there would be a small risk of paralysis and a minimal risk of death. Of course, I am a negotiator, so I always ask about options. When I posed that question, he emphasized that the only viable alternative was to go home and probably die. It seemed like there was no choice; I opted for surgery.

Since I was on painkillers and had gone through a life-altering experience, it took me awhile to grasp what was going on with my body. I knew it was serious but did not realize how severe or symbolic. The words *major artery* hit me. My aortic wall was weakened. My heart had to work harder to pump blood. I needed my blood to flow freely in order to stay alive. Friends consistently reminded me that my situation was major and that I was not comprehending the extent of it all. I wanted to live. The doctor inserted a few stents and a wire mesh to make sure the aorta was repaired.

After three weeks, I came face to face with my own mortality. I realized I wasn't going to live forever and, if I were to make my contribution to society, I needed to get on with life. That was followed by a two-day pity party. I cried, screamed, sniffled, and had intense conversations with God. I said, "God, if you're not going to answer my prayers, then take me." A few days after my pity party, it came to me that, if I am to live my purpose, it is all up to me. I have to tell my story. I must share who I am. I have to speak to the world. I also realized I had not done it already because I had feared what people might think or say. No matter what, it was still all up to me.

> **I Am a Powerful Force of Love and of Light!**

I remembered that I wanted to serve my purpose—to teach people light and love—and reminded God that my mantra is "I Am a Powerful Force of Love and of Light."

So how does my aortic aneurysm fit into living from within? In my world, I accept the maxim, "As within, so without, as above, so below." I also believe in the connection between mind, body, and spirit. In other words, everything is connected. If something is going on in my physical body, then something is also going on in my emotional, mental, and spiritual bodies. In my case, the blockage in my blood flow was connected to my holding back on sharing love in my life—not just romantic love, but love for all human beings.

This is quite fascinating, especially since I say my purpose is to teach light and love. I realized that I could not teach light and love if I was blocking either of them.

This book is based on my inner spiritual journey, which in many ways is intertwined with my religious experiences. Please note that any references to the Bible are from the King James version.

My Spiritual Life: Who I Am

From the time I was a very young child, I felt a closeness to Jesus. I always felt that Jesus was my friend and brother, and so I would have daily conversations with him. As a Catholic school student, I cherished my studies in catechism. The conclusions I drew from these teachings set the framework for my spiritual life. I became grounded in living a godly life.

During my teen years, I learned to lean on prayer for my academic challenges and successes. In high school, before every report card, I prayed and, more often than not, received As. Of course, I must not have prayed about physical education or science because I don't remember ever receiving an A in either of those subjects.

As I matured and became a young adult, my world became focused on my friends and social life, and on establishing myself as a mother and professional. There have been many who have crossed my path to help me on my journey. As a young child, I was helped by Jesus and the Blessed Mother. They were at the center of my prayers and conversations with God.

As I grew older, my mother was my constant teacher. When we were alone—at home or riding in the car—she allowed me to ask countless questions. She was the epitome of sainthood, a devout and magnificent angel who showed goodness and kindness to everyone. A true nurturer, she had the innate ability to bear fruit, not only as the mother of seven offspring but also as an individual who touched the lives of many children and adults alike.

I have had other teachers through the years. All of them, like my mother, have transitioned. They came into my life at a point when I needed to be touched by the hand of God, and God sent them in. In 1984, Pat Reese made me aware of my discipleship. She was a presenter at the Spiritual Frontiers Conference, an annual event that is now the Southeastern Spiritual Conference. She was a gracious, luminescent spirit, a light-bearer. It was during her class that I made a contract with myself to walk the path of light and do the will of God. Pat was the one who issued certificates of discipleship. I first attended her classes with a friend, who had also been thinking about going. We paid our registration fees and drove thirty minutes to Guilford College in Greensboro.

> **Walk in the light and understand Spirit!**

This conference literally changed my life. It not only motivated me, it helped me recognize who and what I am. Classes were held in spiritual healing, discipleship, enlightenment, developing your intuition, and living your purpose. I felt like I had died and gone to heaven. The teachers and attendees were all filled with love. I could actually feel the presence of God.

Among others I met at the conference who also had a major influence on my spiritual evolution was Vashti Edgerton, a woman of astounding magnitude. Around 1984, she came into my life, also as a teacher. Vashti was almost in her nineties when I first met her. At first glance, I knew we had a powerful connection. She taught me that God and I were one, and together we could do anything. Vashti was a highly evolved soul who held classes at her home, teaching others to walk in the light and understand Spirit, plus everything else that is beyond the physical—the metaphysical.

Another woman from the conference whom I cherished, both as a sister and a friend, was Jean Sowers. She had her first stroke and heart attack a year to the day after her beloved husband's death, and she transitioned in 1998. A point of light and love, Jean influenced the direction of my life in ways she never knew. I first met her when I was led to visit her office. She was the office manager for a renowned holistic psychologist. On the shelves in the waiting room were copies of *Daily Word*, published by Unity. I was familiar with it because my mother subscribed to it when I was a child. This led us to many conversations, allowing us to eventually become close friends. On Sundays, my son Christopher (then about ten years-old) and I attended meditation sessions at her home. During summers, she and I worked together in the healing center at the Spiritual Frontiers Conference. Jean was always exposing others to a higher way of thinking. She led me to seek the truth about who I am, to know "I am that I Am." This led to my awareness of inner guidance.

In 1990, I signed up for rebirthing classes. They were sessions set aside for deep breathing. It was really a form of yoga. Prior to the breathing exercises, we spent a lot of time processing. The facilitators were excellent at helping us dig deeply to identify the fears and beliefs beneath our issues. Many of us cried after recalling the events that led to our trauma. It was the most intense therapy I had ever experienced. These classes helped me hear my inner voice. Of course, I had been learning to listen to this inner dialogue for several years. I soon discerned that these conversations were between me and my Higher Self or God.

When I was a child, my mother wanted me to be a nun. I would have loved that, but nuns don't have children. I wanted children—seven of them. Fate would not have it. Though I had five pregnancies, I only gave birth to two, and I am so grateful for those two. They are the epitome of my success as a human being. Though I did not know what I was doing as a parent, I prayed a lot. My two children are the manifestation of powerful prayer. Because I was blessed to be their mother, they learned meditation, the magnificence of manifestation, how to share and be loving human beings, the value of knowledge gained from reading and research, and many other things. They are my greatest gifts. I thank the universe for them. They learned that Spirit lives within them and will always be there for them. The spiritual world I pursued was within me. I was in this world but not of this world. And spiritual teachers confirmed that for me over and over again.

> **The spiritual world I pursued was within me.**

When I was age twenty-five, my own mother passed. She was sixty-three years old. My whole world changed. I would say this was a major pivotal point for me. It changed my life and changed my focus. It put me on a whole different path. My values completely shifted. I remember many conversations with her after her transition and realized there was a void inside me. I felt empty. No matter how many TVs I bought or how large my house was, I still felt empty. One day I sat up and realized that it was not the things that completed me, it was the food that fed my soul. I quickly recognized that material things didn't fill that empty space. The only things that gratified me were prayer and spirituality. I embarked on a lifelong pursuit of a spiritual life. For many years after my mom passed, she constantly taught me, bestowing upon me her wisdom and love. It was as though higher forces placed me in the flow of life, creating opportunities for me to live and learn. It was as though I was getting a PhD in universal law. I seemed to have no control, no management over my parenting, finances, or relationships. It seemed God was taking over my life and putting me in situations to facilitate my inner growth.

Several profound experiences occurred immediately after my mom passed. I was taking classes at the University of Maryland in College Park and living in Baltimore. After my last evening class, I would go to the library to do research. That meant that I was driving home late, at midnight. It was actually too late to be driving up I-95 alone. One evening, I was intensely missing my mom and suddenly felt her presence with me. I literally saw her sitting in the passenger seat beside me. This was the first of many times that I saw or felt her with me. As time passed, I had similar encounters with my mother. It was as though she had come to me to teach me, protect me, and raise my awareness.

Another opportunity to expand my consciousness came when I attended a Cursillo, a Catholic spiritual retreat designed to advance one's spiritual journey. It's a long weekend of prayer, meditation, conversation, Reconciliation, and Mass. My Cursillo was a deeply fulfilling experience that helped me submerge myself more intensely into my inner self. Though not evident on the outside, the changes I experienced were certainly mind-boggling to me. I emerged a new person, intent on living my life from within and being at one with this mighty Power that lived inside me. It was at this Cursillo during Reconciliation that I stated, "I want to walk and talk like Jesus." What was I thinking? As soon as I spoke the words, I thought, *What a crazy thing to say! Who could actually do that?* Spirit led me to make that statement, and Spirit would lead me to many other opportunities—to learn, to explore, to broaden my perceptions, and to learn to live from within.

This life has been quite an adventure ever since.

Intuition: Listening to the God Within

What is God?

Much of the confusion and angst about God is that we all have a different opinion of what God is. For some reason, many of us grew up thinking God was an old white man sitting on a

> When I surrendered, God put me in situations that facilitated my inner growth.

cloud. As we grow older, many of us think God and Jesus are synonymous, and they are, but no more than each of us is God. I think of Jesus as my brother: incredibly powerful and wise. I think of God as the great entity that watches over us. In the Holy Trinity, we have Father, Son, and Holy Spirit. Father/Mother God, to me, is a being that is much more than I can honestly encompass. I have begun to realize that God may be the essence of all our elders and great wise people who have roamed this Earth, a Magnificent Power or Force that is there for all of us at any time. I realize that I must not limit God, as many of us try to do. How could God be limited? I like that Alcoholics Anonymous and other similar groups, such as Emotions Anonymous or Narcotics Anonymous, refer to a Higher Power. Some groups mention a Higher Self. I like these terms. They indicate that there is something much greater than ourselves in the Universe that we cannot begin to fathom or comprehend. But it does exist. It must exist. Otherwise, how could we explain how babies are conceived and born or how the grass and other parts of nature grow? How do our bodies function? We did not create them. There is so much that is Divine on the planet that we cannot understand. To me, it is all mystical. Though we try to intellectualize, the answers are much bigger than we are. We can find solutions by going within, where the answers really are.

Many of us live from the outside in. Our society and our schools teach us to do that. We depend upon our intellect to make our decisions, small and large. It's not surprising, since science is the accepted basis for understanding everything. We are taught to base decisions on our thinking, on formulas, on proven research. The truth is that we don't have enough awareness to come up with sound conclusions. We don't have the full picture or the breadth of knowledge and understanding that help us make sound decisions with foolproof outcomes. We try. We may bring in experts and reliable research to support us, but still we don't have the understanding of all the factors that could affect our choices.

Many segments of our society rely on intuition or Spirit (if you want to call it that). Artists, including writers, sculptors, visual artists, even architects, builders, and landscapers, rely on their inner strength for guidance in creating their work. I often visualize that a muse is sitting above their shoulders helping them produce wonders. An artist friend of mine once painted a picture of great hands reaching down to empower a strong robust man in carrying his load. This was the artist's perception of where this intuition, his power, originates.

Though not popularly accepted, going within for answers, whether through meditation or simply asking for quick answers, can have profound consequences. When I lose something, I always get quiet and ask, "Where is my…?" Almost always, it immediately appears. When I want understanding on how to do anything, I ask, "How do I do this?" Even with writing, I ask for guidance and the words miraculously come to me. I also ask for help when I go out looking for a new car or when I write an agenda for a meeting.

Before I start my day, I sit down for quiet meditation and, once I get quiet, information flows to me that helps me move through my day. It's not always a wise thought, like *Be kind to others*, but it may simply be *Turn off the stove*. Whatever the message, it is something that is helpful to me as I go through the day. Sometimes after meditation, if I have an important phone call to make, the conversation goes exceptionally well and what I want from this discourse comes to me, usually with surprising endings. Almost always, I end my meditations with "Where do I go? What do I do? What do I say, and to whom?"

Marianne Williamson writes in *The Gift of Change*, "Following God's way is not so difficult as it is different. What is difficult is retraining our minds, getting over our resistance to thinking in such a different way than we have been taught. If in fact our only function is love and forgiveness, then the entire world as we know it is wrong. And it is. The thinking of the world is 180 degrees away from the thinking of God."

Going within for answers can have profound consequences.

My fascination with meditation began in 1976 when I registered for a yoga class. My desire for the class started after I had my second child and wanted to do stretching and toning. The practice presented much more to me than I expected. It offered me a lifetime tool that supports and inspires me at every turn, so much so that my second child developed a similar inclination towards meditation. He participated in meditation classes at a very early age and joined me in similar groups through the years. As an adult, he still meditates and has taught his young sons to do the same. I am so incredibly grateful that God led me to meditation, a tool that all can use for their emotional, mental, spiritual, and physical health.

The key is that, in the midst of that silence, we tap into a sacred space; we connect to God, Spirit, or whatever word we use for Divine Power. It is that Force that works in our favor. As we grow in our search for inner direction, we begin to sense it, manifest it, feel it. As we do so, it becomes an intermediary that brings to us what we desire.

Intuition presents itself in many ways. Have you ever thought about someone and he or she then appears or calls you on the phone? This happens to me always—sometimes within seconds. I remember many years ago I had just gotten my hair cut in a new style. I was moving around the house casually, thinking about a friend. Serendipitously, she appeared at my door, saw my short hair, and excitedly said, "Wow! I was just wondering how you would look with your hair cut." That couldn't have been an accident.

Another example is getting a vision and it occurs. Very similar to the above example, the difference is we don't put words to it. The picture just comes to us in our minds. We often don't even know what it means. There have been times when I have seen faces in my head. I cannot remember ever seeing this person but later—maybe years later—I meet that person. Suddenly, it becomes clear that I have seen that face before, not face-to-face but in a dream, or a vision.

Have you ever looked up suddenly and seen someone looking at you? You had a reason for looking up, probably because you felt something. It happens to me often. I look up and another person is staring at me. Likewise, when I stare at someone for an extended period, then that person turns around and sees me watching him or her. I feel embarrassed. But the other person also feels my eyes on him or her. We feel intangible things. We perceive things that cannot be explained. Is this intuition?

Another example of how we experience intuition is thinking a thought and someone else says it. We easily accept this when twins do it or when couples do it. Often, people who have been close for a long time end each other's sentences, but we think less of it when people who are not twins or couples do it. On some level, we connect. This is being "as One."

Our minds are enormously powerful; they are not solely intellectual, as many of us think, but are connected to a higher place. *The Oxford English Dictionary* defines *mind* as "the element of a person that enables them to be aware of the world and their experiences, to think, and to feel; the faculty of consciousness and thought: 'as the thoughts ran through his mind, he came to a conclusion.'" Also, *Oxford* suggests synonyms, such as brain, intellectual capabilities, reasoning, and other similar words. Similarly, the *Cambridge Dictionary* defines *mind* as that "part of a person that makes it possible for him or her to think, feel emotions and understand things."

We are all One!

In contrast, the Social Transformation Project, founded by Robert Gass and Jodie Tonita, incorporates mind and heart into their Wheel of Change Theory, which states that "to create true and lasting change—transformation—we must work with all three domains of human systems: hearts and minds, behavior, and structures." They define hearts and minds as "[o]ur hopes and dreams, thoughts and feelings, what we believe is possible or impossible; the ideas, perceptions and beliefs that shape our experience." In American society, we tend to think that our minds are separate from thoughts and feelings and neglect the idea that they work together. Mind is vastly different than our brains and our intellect, and more connected to our hearts. Our brains are physical, structural parts of our bodies; our minds are not physical but relate to our consciousness, our creativity, our uniqueness, our intuition.

We are so intricately connected that there is no way we can legitimately deny it. The expression "We are One" is not an idle statement. We are so integrated as human beings that there is no reason for us not to understand each other. In fact, even when we disagree or are in conflict, we each contribute to Oneness in a subconscious way. There is something for us to learn in a powerful fashion. Being conscious means that we acknowledge the connection and do what we can to figure it out. We question, "Why am I experiencing this? What can I do to resolve it?"

For years, I did intuitive readings, sitting down with another person and tapping into that person's energy to let the person know what I saw or felt about particular situations in his or her life. People would come to me when they had concerns about the course of their lives: relationships that had gone amuck, personal items that were stolen, people who had disappeared. I would tune into their energy fields, and then either hear words or have feelings that I interpreted into words. At times, there were simply symbols that meant nothing to me but were truly clear to the person in front of me. It took me awhile to feel comfortable with this process. I started because people began asking me to do it. I did not know I was intuitive enough to help them, but apparently other people saw something in me that I did not at the time. Little did they know they had much of the same ability as me. One significant point is that we are all intuitive. People go for readings to get answers. What they forget is that they already have the answers. The answers are there, simply for the asking, but sometimes we just need confirmation.

Hearing and listening are within. We must go into our quiet spaces to do so. Hearing takes practice. The more we do it, the better listeners we become. As we master this practice, we let go our tendency to think through our answers. We become more adept at hearing that soft, still voice. It is a very quiet voice we begin to hear. For me, it's not words, it is feelings—not emotions, but it is like someone whispering to me, then I discern what the person is saying. This is a difficult concept for people who have lived on the outside, on the surface, all their lives. The beauty of it is many of our decisions are made by listening to our inner guidance, yet many of us do not know it.

EMPOWERMENT: KNOWING THE DIVINE

Empowerment is knowing that the Divine lives within and allowing it to give us strength. The greatest power we can have is that which comes from inside of us. Some of us call it God, others call it Allah. There are many names for this inner voice, yet learning to listen to it is ultrapowerful.

> **Empowerment comes when we listen and hear answers to our questions.**

Most of us pray. There is no doubt that we know to do this. We learned as small children to get on our knees, press our hands together, close our eyes, and ask for help. The task we are not taught to do is listen. Many of us have learned to meditate. Meditation quiets us down and forces us to listen to the stillness. In that space, we get messages that we wouldn't necessarily hear otherwise.

The empowerment comes when we listen and hear answers to our questions. Sometimes there's no question. Sometimes we simply hear information we didn't know we needed. Usually, I sit down in my quiet place before I leave home each morning. Sometimes it's only for five or ten minutes. Sometimes it can be an hour, but always I am able to clear my busy, hurried thoughts and hear things that are significant, such as *Check the fireplace, and turn off the fire logs* or *Remember to get your cell phone*. I find it amazing. Meditation often helps me remember where to find an item I have misplaced. It also raises my consciousness, so I am prepared for anything I encounter during the day.

My first experience with this was when my sons were young, perhaps ages nine and fourteen. I was looking for something for them, not sure what that would be. Maybe crayons. I don't know, but I remember that I searched and searched all over and became exasperated. I finally stopped and asked for Divine Guidance. I asked, "Where are the crayons?' and they appeared. This happens almost every time I ask. It has happened with searching for keys, for a piece of mail, for shoes, anything, including important papers. The key is to ask and have faith.

Jesus said, "…greater works than these shall he do" (John 14:12) Our greatest empowerment comes from living from within. We forget that the outer flesh is not who we are. Who we are within is our essence, our substance. This spirit is the *all* of us. It is where our thoughts, our feelings, our aspirations, and our being lie. We don't realize that with this power, we can move mountains. We have all our answers there. The power of prayer and visualization is undervalued, and yet it is quite simple. There is a straightforward formula for its success.

When I pray, I ask for what I want. It can be for a bill to be paid or for advice on how to approach someone with a difficult conversation. I say the prayer, then feel the Holy Spirit within me. Afterwards, I claim the answer. It also happens with simple things like wanting a material item. I ask for a report to be written, *and it is*. Or I ask for a car, and it appears. Years ago, I needed a new car. I simply asked that the right car be sent to me at the right price, *and it appeared*. It was a metallic blue BMW. Of course, it was a few years old, but it was a great car that I drove for many years.

Another magnificent gift of meditation is hearing the words to be used in a speech or when writing a document. The

> **Meditation helps our spirits, our essence, our auras expand.**

words simply come naturally. Recently, I spoke to a group, describing services that a volunteer group, of which I am part, had delivered to the community. I only had three minutes, yet I had written out an outline with specific details. Before I started speaking, I asked for Divine Guidance. When I started speaking, I never once looked at my notes. I always ask for guidance before I speak, whether it be three minutes or forty-five. Spirit always comes through.

An added benefit of meditation is that our spirits, our essence, our aura expands. It touches everything we touch or encounter. When we become aware of the invisible or accompanying vibrations, we can feel the magnificence of this etheric body that we are. It becomes huge, touches everyone, and brings them into our powerful space. Until we experience meditation or our inner power, these words sound insane. We do ourselves a disservice by not allowing ourselves to experience this majestic occurrence.

This experience in its most powerful form is sometimes called Nirvana, a Buddhist term, which means a place of peace and joy, a transcendent experience, an enlightened state. It may be what we are all seeking. The poem "Eldorado" by Edgar Allan Poe also suggests that there is such a place.

Dothula Baron

Gaily bedight,
A gallant knight,
In sunshine and in shadow,
Had journeyed long,
Singing a song,
In search of Eldorado.

But he grew old—
This knight so bold—
And o'er his heart a shadow
Fell as he found
No spot of ground
That looked like Eldorado.

And, as his strength
Failed him at length,
He met a pilgrim shadow—
"Shadow," said he,
"Where can it be—
This land of Eldorado?"

"Over the Mountains
Of the Moon,
Down the Valley of the Shadow,
Ride, boldly ride,"
The shade replied,
"If you seek for Eldorado!"

Poe doesn't call it Nirvana. He calls it Eldorado. I see them as the same. When seeking Nirvana, or Eldorado, we must also remember timing. Usually, events happen in the right order. Sometimes we ask for what we want at the wrong time. We have to experience occurrences in a certain order. If not, we move from failure to failure. Yet there is no such thing because there are lessons to be learned often before we can manifest our good. For instance, before we can manifest our life partner, sometimes we must learn how to love ourselves so we can be happy with that person. With each relationship, we learn more and more about ourselves. To paraphrase a famous saying, we must learn from our experiences in order to avoid repeating them. So those learning opportunities are powerful and often painful, but very valuable.

Parallel to timing is Divine Order. If we believe in God or a Higher Power, we must also recognize that what we are requesting must be ordained by that Power. So often, we ask for things that are not in God's timing. We may ask for a new job but have not yet learned lessons from the current one. If the lesson for us in the present situation is to learn to control our tempers, then we will usually stay there until we do. The lesson may be to get closer to our Divine Source. My experience has shown me that there is something greater than me, something I am part of—not separate from, but a partner with.

> **We must learn from our experiences in order to avoid repeating them.**

Divine Love

One of my favorite affirmations is, "Everything is in Divine Order." I go back to Romans 8:28: "And we know that everything works together for good…" Remembering these two ideas helps us to get through tough times more easily, knowing that at the end of the storm is a silver lining. Either we rise to a new emotional or spiritual level or we rise to a new intellectual or physical level. In other words, we may achieve something we have worked for on a physical level or we learn a valuable lesson that helps us in future endeavors. I call this "living in the is." As I write this phrase, I feel ultimate enlightenment. The *is* is a state of being, of living in the presence of God. When we are constantly in God's presence, we know we are always protected and provided for. It's as though we have risen in our awareness but, more importantly, we have attained God awareness. We may feel weightless. We are living from our Higher Selves, not our physical bodies.

Many years ago, several years after beginning to meditate, I went into a meditative state and had the most magnificent experience I have ever had. I began to sense God's presence like I never had before. This was not a visual encounter; it was a sensory one in which I felt "up close and personal" with a powerful force, an experience so profound that it changed me forever. I realize that I only need to call on this presence to be with me, to guide me, and to protect me. In the Unity Church, there is a prayer that goes, "The light of God surrounds me; the love of God enfolds me; the power of God protects me; the presence of God watches over me. Wherever I go, God is, and all is well!" This is an affirmation of faith and confirmation of my mantra: "I am a powerful force of love and light." I walk in light and live in love. That's the only way I know.

Of course, I'm far from perfect, and I'm learning with each passing day, but I know we are more powerful than we realize. When we recognize our gifts, we will have a peaceful world.

Life on the earth plane is a state of constant growth, hopefully. We, as a people, are here to realize that, to learn that we are destined to evolve. We are destined to become one with God. That is our purpose on this earth. Everything else is an illusion. Life isn't about becoming a bank president or President of the United States. It is about growing in love—with ourselves, with other human beings, with God. It is about learning how to acknowledge our shortcomings and healing them, growing from them; learning how to forgive ourselves and others; and loving unconditionally. Too often, we get caught up in the challenges of life, when really our task is to let go and let God.

LOVE: THE MOST POWERFUL FORCE

Love is the most powerful force. "Faith, hope and love, but the greatest of these is love" (1Corinthians 13:13). I am of the opinion that love can change the world. Love will change the world. I believe that we are moving in that direction. In spite of outrageous behavior being exhibited these days—towards ethnic groups, races, religious sects, genders, and so on—we are moving in the direction of being a more loving society. Many years ago, I heard a speaker say that the Earth was intended to be a planet of love. All the powers that be are assisting us in that endeavor.

The violence, the anger, the aberration, the inhumanity to man—all are working together against Divine Love that is committed to sustaining a world of harmony. Love is the greatest power. Love is who we are at our deepest source, the center of our beings. Every human being, no matter how damaged at his or her core, is a luminescent being. Humans just haven't learned how to magnify their essence.

> **Love will change the world!**

Forty years ago, I felt continuously depressed, dark. I did not know how to let myself sparkle. I usually walked around with a sad expression. I was sad and extremely insecure. One day, after stepping out of my comfort zone, I started beaming. I was approximately thirty years-old and had felt led to volunteer for a few women's projects at the YWCA and with the Council on the Status of Women. I was thrilled to begin something new. I started letting my inner light shine. To be honest, I do not know what triggered this behavior. I do know that I had begun to take risks and say yes to my gifts and talents. I allowed myself to glow and grow. Subsequently, I became a new person. The truth of the matter is that we are constantly renewing ourselves, but most of us don't allow ourselves to metamorphose into that new person. We stay stuck in our old familiar patterns and selves.

The purpose of life is to grow into the beings that God intended us to be. Most of us limit ourselves. We stop growing because we are afraid to take chances. Either our fears take over or we allow our families or society to limit us. We think we will be poor or be homeless. The truth is that many successful people were poor or homeless before they achieved their dreams. There are many entertainers who are now wealthy but went through years of sleeping in their cars or sweeping floors while pursuing their dreams.

I know of one exceptionally talented actress whose mother quit her job, sold her house, and drove across country so her daughter could attend a performing arts school. For years, they sacrificed endlessly so she could audition for roles, meet the right people, and write and produce her own film productions. Slowly but surely, life changed. Producers and directors saw her talent and cast her in roles that have made her a star. She is not yet a household name but she is surely getting there. She and her family have claimed it. She is becoming that household name, after having gone through many years of smaller roles and commercials. The lesson here is that metamorphosis happens, but we have to believe in ourselves enough to move forward, to pursue our dreams.

On an even smaller scale, we can shift our personalities. As the saying goes, "Fake it until you make it." We can decide that we want to be personable, or we may want to let our inner lights shine. It can happen. When I was in my early years—childhood, teens, twenties—I had a very dark personality, very drab, too serious. In all my childhood pictures, I look sad. I seemed to have a hard time smiling. Then when I was about thirty, maybe twenty-nine, I decided to change my life.

I went through what astrologists call a Saturn return, something we all go through about that time in our lives. According to astrologists, Saturn returns to the sign it occupied at our births. We get the opportunity to let go of old behaviors and start anew. As for me, it was a time when I divorced, moved to my own apartment, and took on the task of raising two sons alone. I also started therapy and began to step seriously into my spirituality. It was a profound time that for me lasted a few years before I completed it. I emerged a new person who realized the magnificent light that is within me. We all get the chance to become new.

Everyone on the planet has the ability to shine.

So, the lesson is to let ourselves move into the light. As we allow the light to engulf and surround us, we become renewed. We may not realize it at first, but soon we begin to recognize that we are different. We are brand new. We become the person we have always wanted to be. This may not be on a conscious level but, if we were to think about it, we would know this new person is someone we always knew we could be. I know. It sounds strange, but it is a fact. As each of us changes, all of us change. The world changes.

Light is the purest form of love. Light is rarely talked about in our society. A small spectrum of us knows what we are talking about when we use the word. When we were children, we sang, "This little light of mine; I'm going to let it shine." Little did we know the power of those words. We had no idea that we were lighthouses, that our presence was a gift of radiance, infiltrating and healing the world. Everyone on the planet has the ability to shine. We each have in us a brilliance, and all we have to do is allow it to magnify. Submitting to this ideal means surrendering ego and negativity. We are bright lights. We came here to shine. If we would all be points of light, the world would transform in a moment. First, we must learn that peace starts from within each of us. *Practice peace!*

If we can, let us think about our energy, our essence, our invisible selves. It's not just within our bodies but without our bodies, surrounding us, expansive. When groups come together to meditate, often the leader will ask them to visualize their energy expanding to the persons beside them and out into the entire circle, filling the room. As they visualize this energy growing, they not only see this power enlarging, but they also feel it.

> **Everyone on the planet has the ability to shine.**

Yet, everything is energy: the chair, the rug, the wood in the fireplace—everything. According to this layperson's definition, all that comes from the earth is energy because it is all made up of atoms and molecules, which in turn makes every thing a living thing. These living things have auras, and auras are sources of radiation. *Merriam Webster* defines an *aura* as an atmosphere surrounding a specific source, or more specifically, an energy field coming from a living being. So, if everything is energy, then everything has an aura, a source of light.

This is amazing, especially since many of us have forgotten about this light or do not know that we are light, a powerful source of energy. Scientists say this energy comes from the sun. We all have access to it. If we only knew this about ourselves, we would hopefully bask in that source. I say this source is what has been referred to as Christ Light.

The energy on the planet is accelerating rapidly to prepare us for a new way of behaving and living. Though it appears that we are moving backwards, in all actuality, we are transforming. We are really completing the cycles begun in years past and readying for full speed ahead toward years of peace and tranquility. Antiquated institutions are being completely altered. Though it appears they are being destroyed, chaos is occurring so that the world can be restructured. Since we will no longer be able to accomplish tasks in the same ways we have in the past, people will have to change with the times. New systems which are developing will allow creative energy to flow from within.

The pandemic caused by COVID-19 is an example of these drastic changes. This virus hit the world in dramatic ways. It started in China, spread to Europe, then to the United States. It hit all parts of world in just a few months. People contracted the illness in extremely high numbers, then started dying in even greater numbers. In the United States alone, total cases were 239,279 on April 3, 2020, and total deaths were 5,443, rising from 53 on March 2, 2020. By March 2021, almost one year later, total cases were 29.8 million, and total deaths were 542,000. In most states, citizens were being warned to stay inside and wash their hands regularly or, if going outside, to wear masks and stay six feet away from other people. There was no cure. Those with extreme cases were dying. Yet many had minimal symptoms and were over them in just a few days. The world was in turmoil, in chaos. But according to chaos theory, a situation may appear to be one way yet ultimately end up another way.

Though on the surface, the picture looked sad and grim, I thought perhaps this was a time for healing physically, mentally, emotionally, and spiritually. I thought it was a time for global cleansing. My mom always said, "God works in mysterious and miraculous ways." Could this be one of those times when God "showed up and showed out?" There was so much wrong in our world that maybe we needed this pandemic to get it all right. This was a time for us to pray, meditate, reflect. It is amazing how much wisdom comes through when we get quiet. We realize how blessed we are how good God is, and that all is well in our souls. Take pleasure in being in God's presence, each of us alone with our higher selves. Love it. Love who you are. Love what you are. Just be. It was all going to be okay. I remembered that everything works together for good, always. So many of us prayed.

As new systems were being developed, our bodies were also being transformed or restructured. As many of us have known for decades, our DNA has been shifting. As we move more and more into the new age, our planet is changing and so are our bodies. Many have noticed that we are sleeping more, becoming more intuitive, feeling strange shifts in our energy bodies. Phenomenal events like COVID-19 have shifted our energy fields and thus our physical bodies and our world. When George Floyd was murdered by police officers in Minneapolis, the protests began on an international level. Amazing and astounding situations were occurring. Peaceful protesters in front of the White House were showered with tear gas so that the President could have a public relations moment in front of a nearby church. A few days later, the mayor of Washington, D.C. ordered the words "Black Lives Matter" posted near a temporary fence that borders the White House. It seemed the whole world was finally understanding the plight of African Americans and other people of color who had suffered so severely for hundreds of years. The Supreme Court even blocked the President from ending DACA (Deferred Action for Childhood Arrivals), legislation which gives undocumented immigrant youth protection from deportation. It seemed as though

God was speaking up and righting the wrongs that this country has waged against black and brown people. Love was expanding.

When I mentioned the wrongs we have experienced in the world—hatred, jealousy, violence, vengeance, narcissism—I also mentioned things being righted. As we have moved through these transitions, we noticed people's treatment of each other changing. People donated millions of dollars for research and equipment, individuals made and donated supplies, and young children raised money and donated it to significant causes. The good that has, and is still, coming out of this travesty is creating a new world.

We are really completing cycles begun in years past.

When I attended Spiritual Frontiers Conferences at Guilford College in the 1980s, one of the speakers said the time would come when we could no longer straddle the fence. We would have to make choices for either good or evil, and that those who chose the latter would have to go to another planet to live out their karma because the earth was intended to be a planet of love. It's time for us to demonstrate love. We are observing now that this is happening. In our United States of America, about half the country sees situations, particularly in our government, one way, and the other half sees them entirely differently. My belief is that this is leading us to love. When Marianne Williamson speaks of love, many people laugh. How can we laugh at the concept of love? Isn't that what Jesus taught: to love others as we love ourselves? We are all one. That is the way to return our planet to love.

Authenticity: Being Who You Really Are

An important aspect of "walking in light, living in love" is living in integrity, balancing our actions and our beliefs. Each of us was created with our own talents and purpose, but instead of tuning in to our authentic selves, we compare ourselves to others, and do our best to follow their patterns instead of our own. We do not realize that we actually miss our mark when we follow someone else's goals rather our own. According to the *Psychology Dictionary*, authenticity is the quality of being genuine and true to one's own values. What a wonderful feeling it is to be true to oneself, to walk one's own walk, to talk to one's own talk. This is when we become truly absorbed in our own path, our journey, and begin to stand out. This is the only way we can achieve fame.

I often think about comedians or other entertainers who were probably told their dreams and ambitions were implausible, foolish. People may not have taken them seriously, until they became wealthy and famous. Then everyone wanted to support them. Another example is the person who wants to be a leader but does not have the talents to do so. That person's gifts may be in drawing or technology but not in leadership, in supervising people, or directing an organization; however, that person may have

> **We miss our mark when we follow someone else s goals rather our own.**

been programmed to want to move up the organizational ladder. The person doesn't realize he or she is impeding his or her progress or cutting himself or herself off from what would be his or her unique form of success. That person's authenticity would be more easily attained by honoring his or her true path, trails that would more likely help that person reach destined levels of accomplishment.

In the workplace, at home and in other parts of community, authenticity can also mean simply being frank and honest about one's expectations and capabilities. An example might be to say to someone who monopolizes your time, "I really need to get my work done. I have a deadline." To a next-door neighbor who is making a lot of noise when you are enjoying your quiet space, you could say, "I'm trying to rest. Could you please turn the noise volume down? It's disrupting my sleep." Faking it and pretending that whatever the other person does is okay is dishonest and lacks integrity. It works against having sincere relationships.

Healing Oneself: Tools for Change

Most human beings have no idea how powerful they really are. We have the power to not only heal our lives but also heal ourselves and others. Through the years, I have taken advantage of many complementary healing techniques and have been terrifically pleased with the power of each.

Meditation and Yoga

What is meditation? What is yoga? How are they different? Meditation is, in my definition, quiet time, in which one is focused on one's inner self and breathing. Yoga is, again in my definition, a spiritual practice that focuses on deep breathing, meditation, and specific body movements. Meditation and yoga presented themselves to me in my late twenties. After the birth of my second child, I decided to take a yoga class as a means of toning my body again. I signed up for yoga and thoroughly enjoyed the experience. At the end of each session, the instructor spent the last twenty to thirty minutes talking us through a guided meditation. I loved it. I loved the peacefulness, the contentment. I became drawn to it, and after the class ended, I began to practice on a regular basis. Of course, it took several years for me to have a meditation session without wandering away from my stillness. It took a while to learn, to get lost inside of myself. Now I meditate every day, though some days I only take five to ten minutes, but I love to spend forty-five minutes to an hour just getting into me. Meditation has the power to change our lives.

Yoga is a technique for becoming One with the Divine. Yoga literally raises one's consciousness and vibrations. Most people know yoga as a five-thousand-year-old practice. That is not true. The origin of yoga can be traced back at least ten thousand years. In fact, there was no singular form or school of yoga back then. Adi Yogi, also referred to as the first yogi, was the enlightened man who brought together all the best forms of yoga practiced in ancient India and compiled them into what came to be known as yoga thereafter. Until then, these were exercises and meditative techniques that people indulged in as a matter of routine.

Ancient yoga aside, there is no single school of yoga or a particular type that you need to endorse. There are various types of yoga. These types are not necessarily classified according to the level of difficulty or complexity. Yoga can be classified into various types simply based on what it does to your body and mind.

Yoga

The basic types of yoga are as follows.

Hatha, perhaps the most common type of yoga in the United States, focuses on posture and body movements. Exercises allow one to move body parts and hold postures while breathing deeply. Hatha is one of the beginning levels of yoga.

Yoga allows us to become One with the Divine.

Vinyasa is another form of yoga that encourages flowing movements and is often practiced with music, almost as a dance form. It requires similar movements as hatha yoga with full control of the body including breathing, but the movements are faster.

Iyengar yoga is another type of yoga where the focus is entirely on detail. The goal is perfect form in which the practitioner holds onto each posture much longer than with vinyasa or hatha. The interesting element about this approach is that the individual is only able to hold onto a posture if the form is perfect. As with all yoga, breathing is essential.

Ashtanga yoga is a series of postures repeated in the same sequence to increase the heat inside the body. It is very rigorous, synchronizing breathing and movement. Ashtanga yoga assists in achieving increased blood flow and heart rate, thus building stronger muscles and body tone.

Bikram yoga is a contemporary form of yoga developed for those who have limited desire to use yoga for weight loss. Bikram yoga has a series of twenty-six poses with two different breathing exercises. An entire session lasts ninety minutes and ideally takes place in a studio or room that has 40 percent humidity and a fixed temperature of 105 degrees Fahrenheit. *Hot yoga* is similar to bikram yoga. Both are practiced in a hot room, but hot yoga utilizes many poses, more than the twenty-six poses used in bikram. This form of yoga is popular with those who want to reach a sweat.[1]

Energy Healing

Several years after learning meditation, I discovered energy healing, or it discovered me. I was blessed to attend a Spiritual Frontiers Conference (now Southeastern Spiritual Conference) in Greensboro, North Carolina. I took a class on *prana* healing. Class members were all gifted in using their intuitions and were powerful in sensing areas in the body that needed attention. I found that they were much more effective in diagnosing

---

[1] "What are The Different Types of Yoga Practices," Celebrate Yoga, Accessed January 11, 2022, https://celebrateyoga.org/different-types-yoga-practices/.

problems than any doctor I had ever experienced. This was amazing. Eight years later in Richmond, Virginia, I attended a level one Healing Touch class. The instructor was amazed at my healing gifts. She was so impressed with my own skills that she offered me subsequent classes *pro gratis*. I was thrilled. As I progressed, I realized I also had the intuition that helped me to understand where people were hurting, and so I was able to act as an agent in their healing.

Acupuncture

It seems as though the Universe was continuing to guide me in the direction of complementary medicine. At no point did I seek guidance in this area, but it found me again and again. When I moved to Wilmington, North Carolina, for some reason I found an acupuncturist. I was looking for an integrative medicine or holistic center and there she was. I didn't see her for long before she moved to another state, but a friend referred me to an amazing acupuncturist who was extremely intuitive and healing. Going to her was like seeing a psychologist or counselor. She was helpful in many ways. I saw her for a few years before she decided to change modalities. I was bewildered and still miss her to this day. Shortly afterward, I found someone else who was just as wise and therapeutic. She helped me through period of gallbladder attacks. After seeing her twice to treat the problem, I did not experience it again until about ten years later when I had moved and was no longer receiving acupuncture. If I had continued to see her, I believe I would not have needed gallbladder surgery at all.

Now I have found another acupuncturist who is superb in many ways. She not only treats my physical ailments, she also helps me in many other ways, giving me guidance about work and other opportunities. I found out about her from my mental health practitioner, who has referred me to other holistic experts. Needless to say, acupuncture works for me.

Chiropractic

Currently, I am seeing a chiropractor and have seen chiropractors for many years who have been extremely helpful to me. Chiropractic medicine is based on the theory that when the spine is in alignment, the body heals itself. They are health practitioners who heal the body, primarily through spinal adjustments and manipulation. Many of them also recommend vitamins and supplements to assist in the body's healing. The most profound experience I had with a chiropractor was when I went to see one in Southern Pines, North Carolina. I had found him by happenstance after an ENT (Ear, Nose, and Throat) specialist removed part of my thyroid instead of my parathyroid, as he told me would. The chiropractor first took a sample of my hair and had it tested to determine where my body was out of balance. He then recommended whole food supplements to combat my physical trauma. It took a year for my body to heal from the thyroid removal. That was five years ago and I have had no thyroid problems since.

Prayer: A Sincere Thought

Prayer changes things. Did you know that any sincere thought is a prayer? There have been a few times when I applied and interviewed for jobs, then afterward said to myself, *I really don't want that job.* Something came to me about the dynamics of the job or the people interviewing me that helped me realize it would not be a comfortable situation for me. It was probably wonderful for someone else. It was just not for me, and thus, I didn't get the job.

Another example is that just prior to the pandemic, I said to myself, I need a few weeks just to stay at home and write. The coronavirus crisis allowed me to do just that, not just for a few weeks but for several months. I say this is being in touch with the Divine. It not only allowed me to put my life in Divine Order but also allowed millions of others to take much needed time to reflect, meditate, write, and so on. We speak the word, and the Universe complies. Often the word is silent—it's a thought.

> **We speak the word, and the Universe complies.**

Connecting with Kindred Spirits

This is an amazing tool. When Spirit leads us to certain people, it is an opportunity to see ourselves, to interact with others who are like our mirrors. We are able to look inside the other and see ourselves. In this modality, not only do we experience ourselves, we can talk in synchronicity, intimately, and generate outcomes for each other that we probably never would have produced on our own. Of course, this occurrence does not come from the head but from a higher source. Have you ever been able to talk to someone and feel like you're on a higher plane? It's a spiritual experience, as though you're talking to God. That is what interacting with a kindred spirit is often like. It's cathartic.

Journaling

Another powerful exercise is journaling. Writing down our experiences is truly therapeutic. Once we recall them and then write them down, sometimes we can see the significance of the details. We are able to process what happened, then the why (the lesson) comes to us. It's much the same as connecting to a kindred spirit. We are connecting to a higher source. The only difference is that in this case, we are using pen and paper, rather than interacting with another human being.

Mental Health Therapy

Effective mental health therapy is similar to the process described above in connecting to kindred spirits and journaling. When the therapist can facilitate the process and allow the client to find his or her own answers, then the process is phenomenal. This happened when I first visited a therapist. She let me talk. While talking, she asked me directed questions, many *who*, *what*, and *why* questions. She never tried to give me advice but facilitated our conversation in much the same way that a mediator would. By the end of the session, I felt elated that I had come to my own conclusions. It just took one session, and I knew the direction in which I should go. I have used this facilitative technique in my counseling and mediation work as well.

I strongly believe that we all have our own answers. It can be greatly beneficial when someone can help us go within ourselves. That is where the solutions lie.

Co-creators with God

This is a topic that many people dispute. I am not sure why, except that many of us refuse to accept our power, our wonder.

If we are made in God's image, then we are God. My experience has taught me that I need God to manifest what I want, and God needs me.

Science of Mind is a spiritual/philosophical movement, founded by Ernest Holmes in 1927. At its core is an affirmative prayer called spiritual mind treatment. The five steps in their prayer process are as follows.

1. Recognition—know that God is all there is;
2. Unification—know that you are One with God;
3. Declaration—state your word for the circumstance you want to manifest;
4. Thanksgiving—give thanks for your word being acted upon by the Law of Mind; and
5. Release— "And so it is!"

The basis behind this prayer is Oneness with God. We cannot create without God, but first, we must acknowledge our oneness.

We are co-creators with God

What happens with most Americans is that we refuse to accept our greatness. What would happen if we removed our egos and realized that we can do nothing *without* God, but we can do anything and everything *with* God? "I can do all things through Christ which strengtheneth me" (Philippians 4:13, KJV).

HEALING THE PLANET, CHANGING THE WORLD

As was stated earlier, the earth was created to be a planet of Love. To get there, we must replace everything *unlike* love with love.

Visualization

We must begin to use our power of imagination, which comes into us from above, flows into the crowns of our heads, and descends into our hearts. From our hearts, we visualize love emanating out into the world. We often think of our imagination as being fantasy. Oh, we believe that children often make up stories about their imaginary friends or tell stories and fairy tales from their imagination. However, imagination is much more than that. Imagination has to do with resourcefulness, ingenuity, creativity, vision. It is a powerful storehouse of knowledge and inspiration.

Visualization allows us to create our inner worlds—as within, so without. All of our experiences come from our imagination. We can use our ability to visualize to manifest our desires. If our desire is to create a better world, then we can begin by seeing that which we want. There is a bumper sticker that reads "Visualize Whirled Peas!" (Visualize World Peace). The more of us who utilize this practice, the more we will see it in our world.

The problem is that too many of us operate in the physical. When there is a problem, we try to resolve it by thinking it through. That can be helpful, but visualization is even more helpful. Our task is to begin to operate from our hearts, sending out love and the powerful energy that goes with it. My personal activity is to feel that love in my heart and transmit it out into the world. Or if there is concern about my home or my car or my family, I exude love into and around them, knowing that they are protected. This same power, this same energy, is forceful, vigorous, intense, and can work wonders.

Metamorphosis

In 1985, I wrote a chap book entitled *Metamorphosis: Or Emerging from the Cocoon*. In it, I shared the path toward fulfilling our life's purpose, and becoming the best we can be. I emphasized the importance of determining our direction, setting goals, taking steps towards those goals, and voila, we are transformed. It takes time; it takes work. We grow.

In the same way, the planet must metamorphose. We are responsible for this change. We can already see signs of the change. More and more people have become passionate about the environment. People are recycling, avoiding use of plastic, advocating for clean air and water, saving the planet. National leaders have become champions for changing our behavior to avoid destroying the plant. University professors are engaged in environmental justice; graduate students are researching farm corporations that are polluting the environment; many people are eating better, avoiding meat or at least eating healthier. Many others are meditating and forming healing circles around beaches, lakes, in parks, in homes. In whatever way possible, we must work on healing the planet by marching, writing letters, calling our members of Congress, signing petitions, holding or attending public rallies, and praying, meditating, and visualizing.

As individuals are changing, the planet will change. The planet is undergoing a metamorphosis.

> **Our task is to operate from our hearts, sending out love!**

LIFELONG LEARNING: SUSTAINING PEACE

The day you stop learning is the day you grow old. Live life to the fullest. There is so much to learn and cherish in this world. Take advantage of it.

An article by Anwar White emphasizes that. He writes that *The Collins English Dictionary* defines lifelong learning as "the provision or use of both formal and informal learning opportunities throughout people's lives in order to foster the continuous development and improvement of the knowledge and skills needed for employment and personal fulfillment." Introduced in Denmark as early as 1971, the term "recognizes that learning is not confined to childhood or the classroom but takes place throughout life and in a range of situations."[2] White further says that "Many educators and parents actually advocate lifelong learning because it is considered something that is crucial in a person's development and growth."

I find that people who settle and only stay within their comfort zones begin to slowly wane and die before their times. When we open up our minds and hearts to new ideas and experiences, we thrive. Life takes on new meaning. We are One with the Divine.

In the Womb

The truth is that we are always learning, even in the womb. We've often heard parents say, "I talk and sing to my baby." I

---

[2] "Lifelong learning," Wikipedia, last modified January 3, 2022, https://en.wikipedia.org/wiki/Lifelong_learning.

once heard one dad say that instructed his baby, while the baby was still in the womb to follow sports and aim to be an athlete. It is believed that babies are cognizant and aware of what is going on around them. Some groups even believe that babies are conscious of what is happening during childbirth. We have memories of the trauma, of whether we are welcomed by our parents, and if there is discord between our parents. A study out of Pacific Western University states that unborn babies are listening to their mothers talk during the last ten weeks of pregnancy and at birth can demonstrate what they've heard.

Patricia Kuhl, author and co-director of the Institute for Learning & Brain Sciences at the University of Washington, concurs, writing, "We want to know what magic they put to work in early childhood that adults cannot. We can't waste that early curiosity." Researchers say that infants are the best learners, amazingly, and learning how they process information can give more understanding on lifelong learning.

> **Help children recognize and develop talents for which they are most passionate.**

Childhood

White believes one of the best gifts that can be imparted to children is to develop and nurture children to be lifelong learners. We want to raise children who are not just knowledgeable but who are also motivated to learn on their own.

Many people know what they want early in life. Simone Biles started focusing on gymnastics at six years-old, and Raven-Symoné began acting at age three. Justin Timberlake began performing at eleven. Some of us may remember Shirley Temple, child actress and later a Congresswoman from

California, who was discovered at three years old. The list is endless and includes not only athletes and entertainers, but also entrepreneurs, scientists, public speakers, and other prodigies. These children recognized what they enjoyed at a very young age. They realized their passion, and someone encouraged and groomed them to become the talents and successes that they were intended to be.

We want to equip children with life skills, such as curiosity, independence, sensitivity to others' needs, expressivity—these are skills that matter as they go through life.

My thoughts about lifelong learning are that:

1. Parents and schools should identify children's interests and strengths while the children are still young.

2. Adults should focus on the child's skills and talents for ultimate child development.

3. Schools and parents should emphasize and enforce training in the areas identified.

When individuals recognize and realize talents about which they are most passionate, they are most inclined to pursue them vigorously and adopt them as lifelong pursuits, thus contributing to areas of lifelong learning.

Adulthood: Letting Go of What Limits Us

When individuals reach adulthood, they have already gone through year grooming by the adult world and through socialization. The innocence and sincerity they had as children has been eliminated and replaced with the world views of the masses. As a child, I dreamed of being an entertainer. I would have been a wonderful actress. In every play in which I performed, I had the lead role. I loved it but my parents thwarted that idea. They insisted that acting was not a stable profession and I needed to find a reliable job, such as teaching. Though education is truly an honorable profession, I was never happy with it. There are many teachers who were born to do that job. I know many of them. One of them was my mother. It was apparent that she loved the students and the skills it took to mold them, but I did not possess the same talent. We must be careful not to limit our children or ourselves.

In the same vein, low self-esteem holds us back. If we have not been encouraged and motivated to be the best we can be, or if we are not told often enough that we have great abilities and promise, then we have a hard time believing that we can do whatever we set out to do. Fears can also limit us. Our fears of failure, of thinking we might not be a success, lead us to believe we could not possibly become the magnificent scientist, great politician, or stupendous musician we dream of being. There is also the thought that we just might succeed. Again, that goes back to fear—fear of becoming all we want to be. The idea might be overwhelming: to see ourselves in the spotlight, to see ourselves shining.

One of my favorite authors and public speakers, Marianne Williamson once wrote:

> Our deepest fear is not that we are inadequate. Our deepest fear is that we are powerful beyond measure. It is our light, not our darkness that most frightens us. We ask ourselves, Who am I to be brilliant, gorgeous, talented, fabulous? Actually, who are you not to be? You are a child of God. Your playing small does not serve the world. There is nothing enlightened

about shrinking so that other people won't feel insecure around you. We are all meant to shine, as children do. We were born to make manifest the glory of God that is within us. It's not just in some of us; it's in everyone. And as we let our own light shine, we unconsciously give other people permission to do the same. As we are liberated from our own fear, our presence automatically liberates others.

-Marianne Williamson, *Return to Love*, 1992

Aging

As we grow older, we hopefully become wiser. Many of us take the time to look back over our lives and assess what gave us contentment and what gave us sorrow. Some people look at what they could have done differently

Your playing small does not serve you or the world.

and proceed to do those things they regretted not doing, like finishing high school or college, using their artistic skills, starting a business, or any number of other activities they were unhappy about not achieving. We can look at aging as a second chance or we can look at it with disappointment. I choose to see it as an opportunity, not a time to give up on life but a time to acknowledge who and what we are. We can fulfill our *Why?* or we can sit down and wonder *Why not?* I know of a woman who, at eighty-three, started art classes. She wanted to paint and, before she passed, she became very well known in her community as an artist. There are many examples of famous artists who became known late in life.

An example is Carmen Herrera, a Cuban female who became renowned at 103 years-old, after which her works went on exhibit at the Whitney Museum in New York City and a few other locations. The secret of her success was persistence. When she was shunned because of her gender and nationality, she continued to persevere and eventually fulfilled her dream. With lifelong learning, we never know when we will achieve, but the lesson is to keep trying, and never give up.

I, for one, went back to graduate school at age fifty. I have always loved learning, so it was another opportunity to grasp more knowledge. I already had one graduate degree, but I just wanted to go to school. I thought it wo help me in my career, and it did. I was working at the time in a mediation center, so I found a distance learning program that interested me. I should say it found me. I am so glad I pursued that program. It taught me so much about conflict and varied world views that contribute to conflict. It was an amazing lesson in relationships, human vulnerabilities, and how to honor them.

While we on this earth, we have many opportunities to learn. As we grow older, we have more time to take advantage of them.

Sex and Intimate Relationships

We honor ourselves and our partners by experiencing intimate relationships with the ones we sincerely, genuinely, and mutually love and respect.

Creating Love

What is love? How is love created? After many years of testing, I realize that we do not create love. If it is sincere, it is given to us. Two people are drawn together through synchronicity, or chemistry as some people call it. Even if there is no physical attraction, there is an unidentified or unseen magnetism. Often, they may feel like they have known each other forever. Whatever the force that draws them to each other, they recognize it.

Some people resent using the word *love*. As someone once said to me, "People overuse the word love. They often don't even know what it means." This friend proceeded to use the term *connection*. He emphasized that people have strong connections to each other. I can accept this analogy. However, we define it, two people are pulled or magnetized towards each other. If they both are willing to accept this attraction and let go of distractions and fears, they may have a glorious life together.

Partners United in Love

They can become partners united in love. When people are united, they generally admire and respect each other. That does not mean they are always blissful together, but it does mean they are committed to each other, whether married or not. Through my life experiences, I have learned that love and partnership ideally are not about physical attraction or sex. They are about connection, as mentioned before. Once a relationship is formed, based on inner connection or chemistry, almost nothing can pull it apart. A phrase that is part of traditional wedding vows goes, "What God has put together, let no man put asunder." All my life I wondered what that meant, when almost everyone I knew had gone through a divorce. Did people not respect the words they had stated during their weddings? I, myself, have done the same. I have taken those vows, and still divorced several years later. How could I have made such a statement and not taken the words seriously? The truth is that the people involved are often not divinely connected. They may like each other's physical appearances, they may respect each other's intelligence, or they may honor the other's character or morals, but none of this is the same as being put together or having chemistry. That bond cannot be destroyed. It is a strong, sturdy, enduring union that no person can tear apart, no matter what.

Sex as Spiritual Practice

Keeping in mind that a relationship put together by God is forever and durable, the sexual part of the relationship is thus spiritual as well. In our society, we are hesitant about discussing sex, yet almost everyone engages in it at one point or another. I am a true believer that children born of parents who are spiritually connected are very special children, born in the light. The love that created them is a mighty force that lasts throughout the course of the child's birth, infancy, childhood, adolescence, and adulthood. Love is a powerful thing. It is a profound, all-consuming energy.

When that genuine, dynamic vitality pushes its way through any situation and out into the world, it permeates all negativity and chaos. This is the greatest gift society could give itself. Subsequently, sex is a spiritual experience.

Julie Piatt, a healer, spiritual guide, and plant-based chef, writes in MindBodyGreen, a media brand that promotes healthy lifestyles:

Connect to your spirituality. Recognize that we are spiritual beings having a human experience—that you were created from a divine blueprint…Recognize sex as part of this spirituality. Feeling guilty or embarrassed? Please don't. Sex is fantastic, wonderful, amazing, natural, wild, erotic, and awesome. With consenting partners and within the realms of both people's boundaries, sex should occur freely…Decide to see your partner as divine. Accept that if you are a divine expression of this force, your partner is too. Yes, that person who annoys you and challenges you to no end. Expand your understanding and surrender all judgment of the person God has provided as your soul mate…Embrace the act of sex as worship of your partner and a sacred representation of the divine—no matter how different you imagine these things to be. You get out of it what you put into it. Exercise you devotion muscle. Fake it until you make it…By holding this highest vision for your partner, you will be loving them into their best expression of their divine design. This is truly divine principle in action. Yes, you are a healer now.

Julie Piatt says it more clearly than anyone I have ever heard or read: "Accept your divinity and express it through love, sex as a spiritual practice."

Conclusion: Valuing One's Worth and Living on Purpose

Self-Love/Appreciation

Self-love is especially important. Many people have not been trained to love themselves, especially in families where parents do not love themselves. In fact, society does not necessarily reward people who genuinely love themselves. Schools do not teach children to love themselves. Self-love is rewarded when we accomplish great things. It takes self-love, and self-confidence, to achieve anything, such as get a job, earn a certificate of appreciation, or attain a diploma, but the reward is for the accomplishment not for the individual's sense of self-worth. Sounds complicated? When we really love ourselves, we can accomplish anything we want. We are able to attract a loving and kind partner, have a flourishing business, initiate a successful community project, or run for public office—and win. In fact, when we love and appreciate ourselves, we can accomplish anything.

Being You—Who God Created You to Be

One of the many areas in which American society fails is that of helping individuals identify their purpose. We each have unique skills and talents, but schools are deficient in assisting students in understanding what they are. Some parents are becoming more enlightened and steering their children in developing those abilities.

Yet many still expect their children to follow in their footsteps, like run a family business, or pursue paths that are extremely lucrative but not necessarily desirable, such as medicine, law, or business.

In 1989, Marsha Sinetar authored *Do What you Love and the Money Will Follow*. Sinetar wrote about overcoming our fears and taking risks. In other words, she was saying that we could accomplish anything if we allow ourselves to. Many of us take a few steps toward a goal, then give up. The secret is to keep going. "If at first, we don't succeed, then try, try again."

My conclusion is that if we are in tune with our God-selves, then we can achieve. If we meditate, listen to the God within, and love ourselves, then God guides us. I once took a workshop in which the facilitator said, "God gave us talents, guidance, and love," so there is no excuse for failure on any level. One thing that happens, even when we recognize our talents, is that we forget to listen. We begin to work our own plan and follow it, without talking to God first. What makes us think we can do it all by ourselves? Because we have not learned to listen and follow God's guidance, we have not understood that we are One with God. We need higher guidance.

After my aortic repair in 2017, I came face to face with my own mortality. I remember that I wanted to live my life on purpose—to teach light and love. With our Oneness with our higher selves, we become who we really are, the being we were created to be. Once we actualize who we really are, then we achieve what we came to earth to do. The world is waiting on us to become who we really are. We begin to live on purpose.

As we continue to heal from the COVID-19 experience, we have the opportunity to shift our thinking and way of life. We have had almost two year to go within, to reflect on our ways of thinking and acting. We can create a new world, a space filled with peace and harmony, a place where we all live in love and in light.

Milton Keynes UK
Ingram Content Group UK Ltd.
UKHW020346210824
447185UK00005B/282

9 781964 982366